MW01670995

When The Bride Is Barren

PROPHETIC INSIGHT TO HOW GOD IS PREPARING HIS SON'S BRIDE THROUGH BARRENNESS

DR. TERRY L. DAVIS

Published by Dr. Terry L. Davis, Monessen, PA

Contact Information: Dr. Terry L. Davis
NOLMFC, 489 McKee Ave., Monessen, PA 15062

Website: www.nolmfc.com

Copyright © 2011, Dr. Terry L. Davis - All Rights Reserved Under International Copyright Law. Contents and/ or cover may not be reproduced *in whole or in part, in any form, by any means – electronic, mechanical, photocopy, recording, or any other* – except for short excerpts for printed reviews, without the express written consent of the author.

ISBN: 978-0-9831908-1-3

Cover Design: Thomas F. Cannon. Copyright © 2011. All rights reserved.
Cover Photo: BigStock © Copyrighted. Used by permission. All rights reserved.

All names, places, events, dates and /or specific situations are entirely fictitious, and entirely coincidental, unless otherwise stated.

All scriptural quotations are from the New King James Version, unless indicated otherwise.

Scriptures taken from the *New King James Version*. Copyright © 1982 by Thomas Nelson, Inc. Used by permission. All rights reserved.

Contents

FOREWARD

WHEN THE BRIDE IS BARREN is a prophetic word to the Church, and very specifically to the body of Christ here in the western part of the world. I pray that you read it, having ***"ears"*** to hear what the SPIRIT is saying to the BRIDE through his servant, Dr. Terry Davis.

In addition, Dr. Davis peels away the initial layer of ***"reproach"*** that so fully covers the concept of Barrenness. Enabling us to discover the true hidden treasure of its value & worth when it comes to spiritual operations within the Kingdom of God.

I anticipate this book being used by God to help save some from making very poor & wrong choices, which could've otherwise led to devastating outcomes. Because it's during Barren times when Satan's lies abound and we are most vulnerable to come into agreement with them.

Dr. Davis further teaches us that God not only uses Barrenness, but at times will actually be the ONE who's behind the ***"shut up"*** womb of DIVINE PURPOSE within our own lives, just as He was with Hannah.

Read it and find out why a God who ultimately calls us to a FRUITFUL place will at times authorize for us to have to pass through a BARREN place to get there! My suggestion is for you to approach this volume by reading it slow and prayerfully.

Don't forget to have your pen in hand as you read it, 'cause you're going to want to mark up the book with side notes. I guarantee it ... I've got my own marks to prove it~

Pastor/Prophet Philip K. Cappuccio
Kingdom Life Covenant Church
Hershey, PA
May 2011

ENDORSEMENT

Dr Terry Davis, in his descriptive way has so poignantly brought to light the characteristics of the true Bride of Christ. This book will not only speak of the processes of God in qualifying His bride, but I believe Dr. Davis, as a prophet, has heard the heart of God and written a timely word for the day we are living in.

I also believe this book is a must read if one would desire to be able to discern what the true bride (body of Christ) should look and behave like.

-Pastor Patrick T Lyons.

INTRODUCTION

Times of Transition

There are some amazing times of transition that involve the Body of Christ, and I believe it is by divine design. I see the Church awakening to this truth now more than ever before.

With the recent passing of Dr. Oral Roberts, Bishop John Gimenez, and Dr. Bill Bright, the departure of these apostles of divine healing, evangelism, and college youth have many within the Church world waiting and evaluating who is willing, or able to pay the price to catch their mantles for this millennium.

We are thankful that Richard Roberts, Dr. Oral's son, and Bishop Anne Gimenez, Bishop John's wife, have embraced the keys to their ministries. However, there are corporate mantles available within this hour.

Many desire to possess and proclaim, "*Where is the God of* Dr. Roberts, Bishop Gimenez, and Dr. Bright?" Yet, God is not just raising up one particular individual or denomination that will grasp the mantles and the messages; but He is measuring a generation for the fitting.

God is fashioning a Bride for His Son, which is willing to be led through these times of transition from being a spiritually bloated Bride; pretending to be pregnant with revival from God, to actually becoming pregnant with the mantle for revival.

Due to our state of shift, there have been various prophetic proclamations of different seasons for the Church; like all seasons they come and go. There appears to be a negative spiritual shift that is hovering over our nation and the Church has the solution to the current dilemmas. The prevailing question on the minds and lips of theologians, ministers, believers and unbelievers alike is, *"What is God doing in the earth these days?"* The answer is simple and yet profound, He is preparing a Bride for His Son.

Recently, during my personal devotion times, God began to reveal to me that all things are occurring in the earth today because He is seeking a certain type of woman (Bride - corporate believers) for His Son.

Out of these precious times He engraved a phrase upon my heart and mind, which I believe was His prerequisite for the approval of Jesus Christ's Bride, which will lead this generation to revival.

The phrase only consists of five words, yet every time, at the conclusion of my personal devotional time, in the middle of worship, I hear those words in my spirit in a tone of mercy and love. This book is what God revealed to me prophetically, when He said, *"When the Bride is Barren!"*

It's my prayer that this book will be one of the prophetic voices He uses for the Church's precise positioning for revival.

Chapter One

God's Quest for Our Barrenness

(Judges 13:1-2)

"And the people of Israel again did what was evil in the sight of the Lord; and the Lord gave them into the hand of the Philistines for forty years. And there was a certain man of Zoriah, of the tribe of Danities, whose name was Monoah; and his wife was barren and had no children."

The late Howard Hughes was one of the wealthiest and weirdest men in American history. His reported estimated wealth and bizarre behavior were well known, and observed by many. Nevertheless, during a sane season while undergoing a battle with mental illness, he was asked the following question by a newspaper reporter, "What is the greatest problem that you, as a man of tremendous means face?"

Hughes reportedly paused for a few seconds, then flashed his famous million-dollar smile, and replied: "To be able to trust those I love which are around me."

God the Father has a similar issue. He is seeking true worshippers whom He can trust with more than His anointing and spiritual gifts. What's greater than gifts from God? There are 13 known gifts of God's Spirit (1 Corinthian 12 &14) but there are two things He values more than them all. They are His name, and who will be His Son's bride.

He allows life's tests, trials and tragedies to find the address of believers who have been stripped and plundered of their self-help mentality to be identified as His Chosen.

The question is, *"Chosen for what?"* The Church has been chosen to be the gateway into His kingdom here on earth. He shared His love with the entire world by giving His only Son, Jesus, as a ransom for our sins. However, only to the trusted, true worshippers has He agreed to share His precious glory (Jn.17:21).

I believe it is safe to say, God withholds no expense for His Son's Bride. The reason that He is doing this for us, is because He is working to bring the Church to a spiritual level of compatibility for

His Son. He will not allow a contentious woman to marry His Son (Prov. 27:15-16)!

Therefore, ultimately He desires to lead the Church into a state of loving submission and spiritual barrenness. Many believers understand and agree with the submission part, but they struggle to accept that God wants His Son's bride barren. But He does. Please allow me to elaborate.

Webster's Dictionary defines this word 'barren' as; ***'a state of unfruitfulness, unproductiveness, and un-profitable.'*** God's goal for believers is to be unfruitful, unproductive and unprofitable in our endeavors void of His approval, presence, and grace.

Whenever humanity, which is made in God's image and likeness, strive to accomplish unity for a cause that is evil or unrighteous, there is nothing that can be accomplished (Gen. 11:5-7).

Some works being done in the name of God are nothing more than a human project, without God's hand upon it. So, He is recruiting prospective brides that could be the kind of companion Jesus

Christ needs. He is not accepting self-made believers.

We get a glimpse of what God is looking for within this hour when we view Jesus' teachings on the Beatitudes, He said, ***"Blessed are the poor in spirit"*** (Matt. 5:3). If we consider the meaning of the word ***'poor'***, along with the word ***'barren,'*** then Jesus' words will produce a definition of barrenness that will answer the question of why God wants the Church in a state of barrenness. When the Church is poor in spirit, needy, and desperate for resources, the Church must look to God for what possessions He has within His kingdom (Rom. 14:17).

The word poor literally means: ***'to be a beggar.'*** Beggars are people who support themselves through someone else's means; unless someone gives to them, they will die.

Barrenness and being poor in the spirit is the first spiritual law for access to the kingdom of God. Blessed are those (sinners/saints) who understand that all of us are spiritual beggars, totally unfruitful, unproductive, unprofitable and dependent upon the Lord's resources for true spiritual life and productivity. Once we comprehend our inability to produce lasting change within our lives by sheer will and a false appearance of unity, then we stand a chance for real revival.

The Battle: God's Quest for Us vs. Our Choices

Therefore, the Church really has difficulty accepting that it is God's quest for us to be spiritually needy, desperate, unfruitful and unprofitable as a prelude for perceiving God's purpose, plan, and vision for our lives. Why is it so hard to believe that this is what God wants from us? Could it be because it seems impossible for the Lord to find us in this state of acknowledged barrenness due to our false sense of pride and self-sufficiency in our own abilities and knowledge?

If this is true, then we find ourselves in a constant battle between God's quest for us and our choices.

God's quest requires us to pick up our cross of self-denial and become believers sentenced to die daily to every imagination that exalts itself against the knowledge of God. Then we must crucify our undisciplined passions.

Unfortunately, many times our choices normally lead us to deny our apparent condition of barrenness. So, we stuff our shirts or blouses, figuratively speaking, with pillows to give the false illusion of being spiritually pregnant with vision and favor from God. We often forget, God does not need us, He chose us.

Since the fall of Adam in the Garden, every human being has the capacity for raw barrenness before God. The daily battle before every believer in this process is how to handle that He has granted us the powerful right to choose our pleasures, but not their consequences.

Seemingly, within this generation, God is endeavoring to show us how imperative it is to be more Christ conscious than the purpose to pursuing life pleasures.

God's quest for us to address our barrenness properly, has arrived at the doorstep of this generation. The question is; what are we going to do about it?

The Faithful Made Able

During God's quest for us there are some that God will use for His glory. As I read Judges 13:1-2, I noticed a pattern that barrenness is the key to blessings. In other words, God does not send an angel to visit the home of some particular priest or some 'potentially gifted family.'

Instead, the angel goes to a barren woman who is nameless in order to conceive God's instrument of change. God takes the most unlikely and impossible situation to produce a solution to Israel's problem. What was their problem? Disobedience!

As you read the historical accounts of the nation of Israel in the Book of Judges prior to chapter thirteen, you will discover the successions of bondage and oppression they were under. This all occurred because of their disobedience to God.

In chapter four, we read about how Jabin, the King of Canaan, had oppressed them for 20 years with an iron fist rule. In chapter six, we discover the story of Gideon. There; we find that the

Midianities had placed the Israelites under an apartheid type of suppression for seven years.

Then, chapter thirteen, we are informed that the Philistines had the nation of Israel delivered to them by God for 40 years.

An entire generation was under servitude and the bondage of the Philistines.

They were in economic ruin because of the plundering of their land and the enslavement of their people. They were discouraged, and their hope for emancipation from their plight appeared gone; also they were convinced that God no longer heard their cry for help.

In the midst of Israel's troubles and spiritual stagnation, God was working behind the scenes, preparing to use someone for His purpose and glory. Verse 2 says, ***"that there was a certain man Zorah, of the family of the Danites whose name was Manoah, his wife was Barren and bare not."***

Another example of this spiritual principle is when David's father Jesse paraded all of his elder sons before Samuel to be considered candidates for the soon to be vacant throne in Israel. Samuel saw the young men and asked Jesse, ***"are these all the sons you have?"*** Jesse's response to Samuel's question demonstrated how he viewed David's potential to be king one day.

He said, ***"There is still the youngest*"** (I Samuel 16:11). God by-passed all the so called ***'able'*** elder sons of Jesse, despite the fact they probably looked kingly or presidential; yet, when David appeared before Samuel, the oil in his horn to anoint the next king of Israel, flowed upon David's head.

God's choice of David was regardless that he appeared unable to fulfill the office according to his father labeling him the ***"youngest."***

The Hebrew word ***'mabow'*** was translated ***'youngest'*** it denotes '***a sense of less than others, or considered inferior'.*** It means more than less in age, but it also implies inferior to the rest of the family.

However, remember they called David from the pasture, where he was productive in protecting and providing for his father's sheep. David was not initially invited at first because his family believed he was unproductive, unprofitable, and unfruitful regarding kingdom issues.

Yet, like other great men and women of God they were qualified for promotion to, or within the kingdom, because of their faithfulness in loving obedience to perform the last task the Father assigned.

It makes no difference if it is an assignment to be an international diplomatic, or a custodian of construction work-site portable toilets. The same Father God who sent you there is the same One who will call and present a new promotional assignment opportunity.

I define the word '**promotion**' for the Christians as ***'God's approval, support, and favoring (Pro) of a believer's direction, mission, and effects (Motion).'*** Our Heavenly Father calls faithful individuals, then, He grants them an anointing of ***ableness*** to accompany their new assignment of promotion (2 Timothy 2:2).

God's search for barrenness within this generation has arrived at your house, and the question is, 'are you barren enough to be used for His glory?'

Chapter Two

Our Memories and God's Promises

Luke 1:5-7

"In the time of Herod king of Judea there was a priest named Zechariah, who belonged to the priestly division of Abijah; his wife Elizabeth was also a descendant of Aaron. Both of them were upright in the sight of God, observing all the Lord's commandments and regulations blamelessly. But they had no children, because Elizabeth was BARREN; and they were both well along in years.'

The late great Milton S. Hershey was a man of failures and great triumphant as an innovator and a milk chocolate candy expert and business man. After establishing a booming business and flourishing community, he and wife Catherine turned their attention to children in need.

At the urging of his wife, and the memories of a lost childhood without proper schooling, Mr. Hershey founded the Hershey Industrial School (renamed Milton Hershey School in 1950 on November 15, 1909).

Today, Milton S. Hershey is the nation's largest cost free, private, co-educational home and school for children from families of low-income, limited resources, and social need.

Their barrenness caused them to help children beyond their days upon the earth. Children's lives have been changed for the better, for more than 100 years. This was accomplished by a woman and man who were acquainted with barrenness.

The story of Zechariah and Elizabeth possesses deep prophetic value for the Church today. As we view their lives within the Bible, they're an inspiration to any individual, couple, church or nation who is waiting on God to do what He can only do—'give life.'

The scriptures are full of examples of God's great instruments of change that were birthed through barren wombs. Some of these instruments were Isaac the child of promise, who was birthed through Sarah's *barren* womb after decades of efforts (Gen. 11:30).

Then there is Joseph, Jacob's son, a type of Christ, birthed to Rachel after her famous cry to Jacob her husband, '***Give me children or else I'll die*** (Gen. 30:1). Also there was Samuel, the great prophet, who was conceived in the *barren* womb of his mother Hannah after much prayer and travailing (I Sam. 1:2).

However, the birth of the forerunner to our Lord Jesus Christ, John the Baptist, possesses strong prophetic relevance to what God is preparing for the Church in this new millennium. The circumstances and the timing surrounding his birth are worth examining in order to get a glimpse as to what God is doing in the Church today.

Working From a Memory

John's father, Zechariah, provides us with great insight into understanding our times of transition within the Church of the *'barren bride.'* Even Zechariah's very meaning of his name speaks to his destiny and our current plight within the Church.

It is interesting that Zechariah's name means '*Memory of God.'* The word memory means ***'The mental capacity or faculty impressions of recalling or recognizing previous experiences.'***

Zechariah, throughout his adult life, and while performing his priestly duties as a member of the Abijah division, were based upon someone else's memory of God. Doesn't that sound like the state of many churches today? Most of the traditions of our day in the Church, both good and bad, can be traced back to memories of God's movements in our Church history within the last century.

Zechariah had the same dilemma, as an Abijah priest, and a direct descendant of the High Priest Aaron. He was apart of the eighth group of the 24 division priest families which King David had divided for continual praise and worship around the Ark of the Covenant (I Chron. 24:10).

Yet, despite his rich historical past, God had not spoken or moved miraculously within Zechariah's family since the days of the Prophet Malachi, for four hundred years.

Similarly, the Church has a wealth of history of great things God has done, and I've divided these memories in three categories. They are (1) The Reformation. (2) The Realization, and lastly (3) The Refreshing.

As a result of these past manifestations from God most believers have remained faithful to serve God, while waiting upon their own encounter with God. Let's look at these past seasons.

The Reformation

The Reformation was born out of the well-known 'Dark-Ages.' God birthed leaders out of the womb of negative Church traditions to become catalysts for change. Men of God like John Huss, and Martin Luther begged to be cleansed from the corruption of religion, and they possessed a personal relationship with the Lord Jesus Christ. The Church was totally influenced and motivated by their faith. They refused to succumb to the traditions and the philosophies of men.

Despite all their accomplishments within the Church, they symbolically cried out to God, regarding their need for more than just a memory within their barren condition. As a result, the revelation of Justification by faith, not works was birthed in the barren soul of Martin Luther.

Then John Wesley and his brother Charles became spiritually pregnant with the divine insight regarding God's process of Sanctification.

They were hungry for more than just a mental acceptance of forgiveness from their sin. They longed to sense the cleansing effect upon their consciousness of past sin. These men of God teachings and holy pursue of God produced supernatural changes with the lifestyle of many Christians of their day.

This was possible because they were barren in their soul to please God. All these great men were faithful to embrace a memory of God, while pursuing their own personal reality of God.

The Realization

Then the Lord led us to a place of Realization, from laity to leadership. By wholehearted pursue of God, the revelation was birthed that all believers have access to a Holy God who requires the same level of Holiness from us all. Therefore, He birthed believers like William Booth, founder of the Salvation Army, a preacher of holiness and deliverance, along with the great expository preacher Charles Finney.

During that season, there were other Evangelists like D. L. Moody, Billy Sunday, Aimee

McPherson who were used greatly to teach and demonstrate that God's desire to be actively involved in the affairs of His children.

They believed that a relationship with God can be based on more than a memory, but a current reality for anyone who desired it.

They refused to live solely off the monumental memories of Moses, Mary and Martha. They cried out for visitations from the Lord in their barren seasons.

The Refreshing

After many years of the Church being in transition from the Reformation, to the Realization periods, it was time for the Refreshing seasons to begin (Acts 3:19). As always God began His search for barrenness. He found believers that were hungry and thirsty for more of Him.

One of these believers name was William J. Seymour, and the other was Frank Bartleman.

The first was a one-eyed Afro-American holiness preacher, who was viewed by society in his day, the early 1900's, to be nothing more then a beast of burden. The Bible scholars, ministers, and pastors believed that people of color, especially Afro-Americans, was void of a soul.

Then the other barren brother is brother Bartleman. He was a gifted writer, Christian missionary, poor, sickly, but an anointed teacher of the gospel. Both men were from different cultures, experiences, and race, but they both were personally barren and wanted more of God.

Brother Seymour is noted to have been the vessel, which God used to birth the great Azusa Street Revival (1903-06) that touched believers throughout America and the world with the Baptism in the Holy Spirit. Then Brother Bartleman read, studied and researched the various revivals of the past, along with the ones during his day. He is known for his historical book entitled, 'Azusa Street.' It is an account of his personal journey, along with Brother Seymour, to arrive at the Azusa Street Revival (1903-06).

In the midst of war, civic unrest, racial division within God's Church, and anointed women were denied the opportunity to minister, or function within their five-fold office by main-line denominations (Eph. 4:9-12). God sent a refreshing to the Church.

This was made possible as a result of the spirit of repentance. It took some believers that were poor, sickly, discriminated against by other saints who cried out of their barren souls and prayed down a refreshing season that changed the world.

Waiting on a Promise

John the Baptist's mother Elizabeth was a phenomenal woman of God, like her husband Zechariah; she also possessed a priestly connection as a descendant of Aaron.

In Numbers 17:1-11, we have the story of the selection by God of Aaron and his household to serve as Israel's first High Priest family.

God tells Moses to have all of the twelve tribes to bring a rod and write their families patriarch name on it. I always wondered why God had them use rods. Rods, staffs, and sticks have something in common. What is it? They are all former branches; they were formerly connected to a tree or vine.

Godly fruit only grows on connected branches (Gal. 5:22-23), and not on rods, sticks, or staffs.

Jesus provides a greater insight to this truth as He referred to His disciples as branches, meaning that they are still connected to Him (Jn.15:1-4).

Nevertheless, God used disconnected branches (rods) to address Israel's rebellion within the wilderness. Out of all the twelve rods, only Aaron's rod budded and blossomed within the presence of the Lord supernaturally.

Out of unfruitfulness, and barrenness, God chose Aaron to be the one which He would bestow the divine destiny of being used as an instrument of change among his peers.

This is Elizabeth's and Zechariah's inheritance and legacy; the selection by God, of someone in her family tree during seasons of rebellion and prophetic silence.

She qualified to be chosen because she was unfruitful, unproductive, and barren within her own gifting and talents just like Aaron, their family's patriarch rod, prior to God's presence saturating it.

Luke's Gospel account describes Elizabeth as, ***"upright in the sight of God, observing all the Lord's commandments and regulations blamelessly."***

Elizabeth was committed to her marital covenant and her relationship with God totally based upon someone else's ***memory of God***. She was determined to remain faithful to Zechariah and the Lord, regardless of her unfruitfulness, and probably feelings of non-fulfillment in her state of barrenness.

Elizabeth is defined as well along in years, married to a man whose prophetic destiny was to serve God based upon a '*Memory of God*'. What an awesome woman of God!

What keeps a woman like Elizabeth faithful to God and a man whom had not heard or seen God within his lifetime? Could it be the fear of growing old alone, infatuation, low self-esteem, or desperation?

I'm persuaded that the answer is "No" to all of the above. Elizabeth's secret to her heavenly commitment, and earthly devotion is revealed within the meaning of her name. Elizabeth's name means ***'An Oath of God.'***

She was a woman who understood her inheritance and that she was an Oath of God. She was not just waiting on her promise; she became the promise over her life in the flesh.

Memories of God are powerful tools that assist us with our faith to have benchmarks of belief; decreeing that if God did it before, it is possible He'll do it again. But, when you understand that you are an *oath of God*, whatever has not been done before, is absolutely possible because it is He who promised (Luke 1:34-35).

When the Church joins with the memories of God, along with a promise of God, we will be able to manifest the miracle working power of God. Zechariah and Elizabeth had to be covenantal related; otherwise they would not be legally allowed to produce a voice of change within a monumental time.

Unfortunately, too many in the Church have been striving, and endeavoring to birth movements, which are results of spiritual artificial-insemination.

We've become tired of waiting on God to honor His promises over our generation, so, man-made scheduled revivals, church merges, not marriages, networks, and fellowships, not ordained by God are being created.

Too many have been created, as opposed to being birthed through barren wombs that understand that they are an ***Oath of God.***

We must not forget that throughout scripture, God never referred to a man as *'barren.'* He identified some as old, but never *'barren.'* Women in scripture symbolically represent the Bride of Christ, while men many times represent a positional view of Christ (Eph. 5:22: Rev. 21:2 & 9).

Zechariah was faithful to a *'memory of God'*, while Elizabeth was faithful because she understood she was a promise of God. It is the Church, the Bride of Christ, that needs to be barren, not Christ. There is absolutely no problem with Christ's spiritual reproductive abilities. However, He needs a bride that knows who they are.

Chapter Three

Mandrakes Are Not Out Dated

Our generation has really become very aggressive regarding the promotion of sexual explicit issues. As the Madison Avenue image makers of many consumers appetite say, *"Sex Sells, and I MEAN ANYTHING."*

Due to this societal craving for self satisfaction and sexual pleasure the advertisements of sexual enhancement products is more than a billion dollar industry. However, prior to the arrival of the current craze of Viagra, Levitra, etc., there were mandrakes.

Mandrakes are yellow apples commonly found in Palestine during harvest time. They normally do not grow any larger in size then that of a nutmeg, and they have a very strong agreeable odor.

The ancients and some Arabs today, use it as an enticement for intimacy among couples during their honeymoon season and beyond. The goal for using mandrakes was to create an atmosphere where newlyweds would feel comfortable in revealing themselves during their honeymoon season, in an attempt to please each other intimately (Song of Solomon 7:13).

Mandrakes, is a symbolic form of worship, it is meant to be used for no other purpose then to create a pleasurable atmosphere that allures the person of our adoration.

The Church's, figuratively speaking, usage of mandrake-worship, too many times has been used for the attempted purpose of spiritual manipulation, as opposed to being a vehicle of our sincere appreciation of God.

When the sound of our praise team, or choir is the greater focus of our worship to the Lord Jesus Christ, we have reduced our worship experience to nothing more then a spiritual exercise void of any true profit.

Worship of God is the language of Love that even the angels can't understand because they are not the redeemed of the Lord, we are!

Mandrake Manipulation

In Genesis 30:1-16, we find the story of two sisters who were married to one man by the name of Jacob. Their names were Leah, which means *'Beauty and Grace'*, and the other sister name is Rachel, which means ***'Lamb'***.

Leah is the older sister, she is one type of the Church; who is not very attractive to this technology generation; nevertheless, she had the favor of God upon her life. She was not aggressively ambitious or self-promoting, but she was committed to keeping Jacob's name and lineage alive within the earth by birthing him sons (Gen. 29:16-17, 35).

However, Rachel also represents a different season of the Church within our Charisma era. She has a different spirit and temperament in regard to her *'barrenness'* (Gen. 30:1).

Like many within the Church, she was jealous over Leah's fruitfulness, and she wrongfully assumed that Leah's childbearing abilities were a result of her usage of love-apples (mandrake-worship) for a personal agenda (Gen. 29:31).

The Church, within this hour, and Rachel share similar attributes. The Church has embraced the view that giftings are greater assets than integrity and honor. Rachel was convinced that her outward allurement was of more value than inward endearment of her bridegroom (Gen. 29:17-18).

This mind-set is clearly seen by the vast number of attendees of believers at conferences, seminars, and workshops that focus mainly upon activating and developing spiritual gifts.

I'm so thankful for the spiritual gifts within my life. Yet, I need the fruit of God's Spirit (love, peace, joy, longsuffering, etc.) in my life or my spiritual giftings could be harmful, and even worst deadly to others and my destiny (see examples of Samson & King Saul).

Rachel the Church is motivated to try to spiritually seduce God into doing what they want Him to do. Her very name, *'Lamb'*, provides a false spiritual connotation of innocence or defenselessness. However, if you ask any pastor, who has pastured more than three years they will tell you those defenseless, and innocent Lambs have teeth and they will bite.

Like Rachel, the Church within this hour is demanding and manipulative (Gen. 30:14-16). When we are not allowing our barren season to prepare us for a deposit from God within our spiritual womb, attempts to try to spiritually manipulate our Master is inevitable.

Regretfully, our worship experience becomes based upon trying to get God's approval of our personal goals, agendas, along with rings and things. However, there will always be emptiness within the hearts of these types of believers because instead of longing to be with God with no hidden agenda, they only call upon Him because they want what is in His hand, as opposed to what's in His mouth.

God created in the first two chapters of Genesis everything, but man, with His mouth. I'm very thankful for His hand, but what came out of His mouth informed mankind of our divine destiny and purpose (Gen.1:26-30).

Leah and Elizabeth were the type of brides who wanted to conceive to please their spouses. Elizabeth was not just an *Oath of God*; she was a wife of godly character and patience. It is never stated or implied in scripture that she ever blamed Zechariah for her long season of barrenness like Rachel did Jacob.

Unlike Rachel, Leah and Elizabeth never wasted their time preparing fresh mandrake for a man-made moment absent of the very favor of God.

Leah's very name; ***'Beauty and Grace'*** did not describe her outward appearance, but her true inner worth (Gen. 29:17). She possessed low-self esteem, and even an inferiority complex, but God visited her womb repeatedly for His glory.

Finally Leah birthed Judah, and Elizabeth, John the Baptist. They both birthed God's instruments of change. Even in time, Rachel would embrace her barrenness from God's perspective and God opened her barren womb and she birthed Joseph (Gen. 30:22).

When this Church generation yields to our barrenness process, we will birth some Josephs.

The name Joseph means ***'To increase, or add to.'*** God wants to use the Rachel Church '*to add*' His favor and voice within this hour.

The seasons of the Leah and Rachel Church were the trailblazers for Elizabeth; a woman who was willing to become her Oath of God.

Chapter Four

Stages of Spiritual Pregnancy and Birthing

During the time of my wife Shelia's pregnancy with our son Desmond, within a few months' people could tell she was pregnant. But, they did not know the exact date, hour or minute conception occurred.

This is also true about spiritual conception and the exact hour of birthing. Only you and God will know when. Prior to spiritual pregnancy, there are stages which must take place. They are: Commitment, Time Alone, Nakedness, Intimacy, Adjustments and Birthing; Let us example them one by one.

Commitment

"Then Esther bade them return Mordecai this answer, go gather together all the Jews that are present in Shushan, and fast ye for me, and neither eat nor drink three days, night and day. I also and my maidens will fast likewise; and so I will go in unto the king, which is not according to the law: and if I perish, I perish."

(Esther 4:15-16)

Esther is an example of commitment to God's cause in scripture. Her selfless statement, ***"If I perish, I'll perish, but I'm going to see the king,"*** was stated with the possibility of being killed for coming into the king's presence without being requested. Nevertheless, she was committed to fulfill her purpose for being placed in the palace.

Christ is searching for such commitment to Him during our barren process. He will not impregnate a bride if He is concerned about her commitment to carry His revival to the full-term.

He is certain that He will not be an MIA (Missing in Action) Bridegroom, for He is totally committed to see His role fully through. However, He is constantly seeking for spiritual wombs and minds that are willing to stay the course of change. His committed disciples are not jumping into every new relationship with false doctrines or religious movements that is fashionable at the moment.

He has watched His disciples over the past decades bark, laugh, and attempt to recall what God stated to them while they were in the womb to discover

His original purpose for their lives, and fall out under the power of the anointing. But too many, when they get off the floor they resumed their lifestyles with no change.

This truth is clearly seen when the soldiers came to arrest Christ; He acknowledged that He was who they were looking for by declaring those famous words, ***"I am He.*** *"* The Bible states that when He declared who He was they all fell backwards to the ground in the presence of the Christ (The Anointing).

However, they were not changed because they still arrested Him, even, after an awesome experience in the presence of God (Jn. 18:3-7).

Thank God for experiences in Christ that glorifies Him and make us draw closer to His presence. He is not looking for experience seekers; He is searching for committed Christians.

It costs to be committed men and women of God. Whenever there is a call from God for commitment, then there is always a call for choice. Only with the right choices can spiritual conception take place.

Then, character can be constantly cultivated by God's spirit and life challenges. The acts of aborting God's guidance and the abandonment of His timing will disqualify many from participating in the birthing of His new revival.

We need more Esthers who will not compromise for the sake of personal comfort or temporary places of influence; but they will be committed to fulfill God's purpose for their lives.

If their ideas, goals, and personal vision perish in the process, they will still press in to see the Kingdom of God (which is God's ways of doing things) expand on earth. If you are not committed, it is a waste of your to time to seek His face.

Time Alone

But when it pleased God, who separated me from my Mother's womb and called me by his grace, to reveal his Son in me, that I might preach him among the heathen; immediately I conferred not with the flesh and blood: Neither went up to Jerusalem to them which were apostles Before me; but I went into Arabia **and returned again unto Damascus. Then after three years I went**

up to Jerusalem to see Peter, and abode with him fifteen days." (Galatians 1:15-18)

Along with our Commitment to carry the revival within our spirit and soul, we have to have Time Alone with God for spiritual conception to occur. As a pastor, there were times when I visit members of my church at the hospital after a lady gave birth. While there, I would pray for the parents and for the baby's well being.

Despite the fact that I was at the hospital and held the child, or even saw the expecting mother at church during her pregnancy, the church and I was not there during conception. This is true spiritually. Spiritual pregnancies happen during time alone with God.

We have rejoiced, supported and benefited from some of the greatest churches and ministries of our day, but most of us were not there when God planted that ministry in the heart of its founder.

Moses and Jacob met God in the quietness of solitude. It is not impossible for God to meet us in the middle of corporate worship or even in a busy environment. However, it normally takes time and it usually happens where and when we spend time alone with God.

The Apostle Paul, after acknowledging God's call upon his life, departed into a place of solitude he stated, ***"but I went to Arabia…"*** (Gal. 1:17). Prior to preaching the kingdom of God, he pitched his spiritual tent in the Arabian Desert for time alone with God.

He received invaluable instructions, redeeming revelation about the Christ, and a time of personal preparation for his destiny.

Paul did not depend upon the other apostles' revelation of Jesus, but he sought the Lord personally. Then when he had a great grasp of Who Jesus is, and what He wanted from him, then he appeared before the other Apostles in the church at Jerusalem.

Yet, prior to going to present his self before the leading apostles to confirm his conversion and affirm his ministry, he spent three years of quality time alone with God. Is it any wonder he was such a spiritually rich reproductive vessel for the glory of God?

Paul's process for impregnation was made possible because his trip to the desert to be alone with God was his way of demonstrating that he was barren and needed God's view point for his life, mission and purpose.

Nakedness

"Neither is there any creature that is not manifest in his sight: but all things are naked and opened unto the eyes of him with whom we have to do."

(Hebrews 4:13)

While in that time alone with God, there has to be nakedness before Him. We must have complete exposure before His presence. We must not try to cover up our pet sins, fears and doubts. Only honesty and openness will make us naked before Him. If the bride never removes her wedding gown, there will never be the opportunity to replenish the earth.

One of the Church's greatest problems today is honesty. We have confused faith confessions, with crisis confrontations. Many are not confronting their personal issues because they have covered them up with motivational speeches and justification for sin in their lives because they are comparing themselves with others instead of Jesus.

Until the bride disrobes of her self-deception, carnality, and religious confusion, God's search for His Son's bride will not end in our generation. There must be a removal of the clothes of heavy callousness from their heart for the unsaved in their family, their church, and their community.

There is a little test that I give myself periodically. I ask myself in an attitude of prayer, 'When was the last time I wept before the Lord?' I must ask myself that from time to time. I believe if I have not wept over my own issues, then I will not weep over the unsaved in my family, church or community for a month.

Sometimes a bit of insensitivity can enter into my heart. This will make me indifferent, and maybe uncaring.

At that very moment I must be honest with myself and the Lord, like the Apostle Thomas. Thomas did not believe that Jesus was resurrected from the dead. He told the naked truth about his spiritual state (John 2:25). However, Jesus did not rebuke him. All He did was provide Thomas with what he needed to believe (John 20:27).

Let us not be like Adam and Eve, who tried to cover their nakedness by using fig leaves (Genesis 3:7). We must destroy our fig leaves of pride. We must never forget that our Beloved is waiting for us to disrobe and enter His presence through our worship.

Intimacy

"Nevertheless I have somewhat against thee because thou has left thy first love."

(Revelations 1:4)

God's created process for natural pregnancy surely can not take place without a time of intercourse. This is true spiritually as it pertains to the vision, purpose and dreams of God. This type of spiritual terminology is alien to most believers today due to the fact that many have left their first love.

There is no way conception can take place from a distance in the natural; neither can it occur in the spiritual realm. There must be a uniting and intertwining with the very essence of God. The current Church age has exchanged our time with God for activities void of God.

We must follow the example of Mary: ***"But one thing is needful: Mary hath chosen that good portion, which shall not be taken away from her"*** (Luke 10:3). God is seeking those who will allow Him to enter their spiritual wombs and pour in His attributes and divine wisdom.

There is a desire within God the Father for us to long to praise, adore and love quality time with His Son daily. This holy longing is demonstrated by us closing the spiritual door to the world, and lay with Jesus in meditation, prayer and earnest worship.

We are like the virgin Bride in the Song of Solomon who said, ***"My beloved spoke and said unto me, rise up, my love, my fair one and come away"*** (Song of Solomon 12:10).

How lovely and precious are those words to our heart when God calls us aside from our daily activities and He tells us to rise up from our normality and come into His presence where there is supernatural peace, and complete refreshing/restoration.

Adjustments

"Enlarge the place of thy tent, and let them stretch forth the curtain of thine habitations; spare not, lengthen thy cords, and strengthen thy stakes." (Isaiah 54:2)

Once the Church becomes spiritually pregnant with the Lord's new revival, there will be great joy, but also a time of adjustments and a divine precision positioning will occur.

Our doctor informed Shelia and I that this is the most difficult time for the expecting mother.

In the natural, nine months timetables for delivery can be nine years in the spirit realm. When the corporate Church reaches this state, there will be a lot of stretching and adapting to new boundaries of responsibilities.

These adaptations and new responsibilities are clearly seen within the kingdom principles of the ***Call of God*** and His ***Commission;*** likewise there is difference between the impregnation of revival and the birthing of it.

Between the ***Call*** and the ***Commission***, there is the preparation. The same applies to pregnancy and birthing. There were 3 1/2 years of pregnancy for the twelve disciples of Jesus prior to birthing the ministry they were pregnant with.

It is normally at this time a woman discovers that being pregnant is a major sacrifice of her total being.

At this stage, the revival within the Bride's womb is truly symbolic of a natural child growing and preparing for the time of manifestation.

The love and protection in the womb surrounds the child; yet he is totally unaware of his potential impact on the earth until the actual birth takes place.

This is clearly seen spiritually when the Apostle Peter did not realize his potential until after his ministry was birthed at Pentecost in the upper room where he was released to lead 3,000 souls into the kingdom of God.

Along with the stretching, waiting and adjusting, God desires for the Bride to follow His instructions. He requires us to emulate the revival we will be pregnant with prior to its birth, this is what God told Samson's parents (Judge 13:4-5).

During this season God will establish uniqueness for proof of its origin. It will be a different revival. Not necessarily void of some of the traits of other great movements of God, but it will be set apart in some areas of it own attributes.

Initially, we cannot separate the revival (the Child) from the Bride because, spiritually, they are to flow as one during this stage.

Also, whatever nourishment the Bride eats the revival receives the same. Despite the fact that the Bride carried, nourished, and protected the revival, it is the Lord's gift to us, not our gift to God. He does not need a revival, but we do.

Birthing

"And the woman bares a son, and called his name Samson: and the child grew and the Lord blessed him." (Judges 13:24)

During the pregnancy, there will come a time when the season of birthing will arrive. I'm convinced that this time God's movement will not be birthed within a particular stained glassed cathedral, church or ministry where religious rituals present no relieving reality to hurting humanity.

The Church's next revival will come out of churches, ministries, and fellowships where covenant relationships have been established and personal discipleship is practiced with new passion.

This kingdom pattern for birthing God's movement is seen clearly in the life of King David's place of spiritual birthing.

He was not birthed as a spiritual movement while serving in his father's house the day Prophet Samuel anointed him (I Sam.16). He was impregnated that day. However, he was not birthed the day when he defeated Goliath, nor was he when he received Prince Jonathan's articles of royalty (I Sam. 18).

David's birthing process occurred in a cave name Adullam. Adullam means *'a place of refuge.'* It was within that cave he was birthed as a movement of God and birthed four hundred men who were formed and fashioned after his kind.

These men were in distress, in debt and discontented with the false outward appearance of revival within their land under King Saul's administration.

They eventually became David's proof he was God's instrument of change for his generation. They became David's famous Mighty Men of Valor (2 Sam. 23&I Chronicles 11).

Notice that David did not give birth while serving in the King's palace, nor within the Tent of Meetings He was birthed in a time of desperation, exclusion and hunger for God's voice and presence.

Another example of birthing is seen in the scriptures as they describe Jesus weeping over Jerusalem prior to His entry. He demonstrates the signs of delivery like an expectant mother whose water has busted (Luke 19:41).

Medical science tells us when an expectant mother's water breaks, from that time on to their actual delivery; the birthing process is most dangerous for the child and the mother.

Due to the seriousness of what He was pregnant with He does not seek the temple of His day for His delivery, or surround Himself with the popular priests to act as spiritual midwives.

As the birthing time draws closer, Jesus chose the Garden of Gethsemane, which means *'Oil Press, a place of pressure.'* He begun groaning and travailing in great agony over the beginning process for birthing a movement that would change the world forever. The Church!

King David's spiritual water broke while wandering and weeping in the wilderness. Jesus' water continued to brake in the garden, but it was fully released upon the cross of Calvary when they jabbed Him in His side.

And as a result *water* and *blood*, two signs & symbols of birthing, they gushed out of His side and the Church of the living God was birthed.

As God prepares us to birth revival, we can't afford to be positioned within the wrong place.

During this season we must walk in accurate discernment regarding those who appear to be close to what the Church is carrying from God.

Some may seem covenantal connected by their works and association, yet they are not willing to share in the painful laboring process.

The birthing of this revival will require much Fasting *(sacrifices*), Weeping *(brokenness)*, and Mourning *(longing)* before it arrives (Joel 2:12).

Chapter Five

The Bride's Children Of Leadership

'And the child Samuel ministered unto the Lord before Eli. And the word of the Lord was precious in those days; there was no open vision. And the Lord came and stood, called as at other times, Samuel, Samuel, then Samuel answered, speak; for thy servant hearth.' (I Samuel 3:1& 10)

Throughout biblical history whenever God determines that the Church needs a paradigm shift in our thinking, worship and behavior He begins His search for a barren womb.

The story of Hannah and Samuel demonstrates such a search and shift in Israel's life as a nation. God is always the author of an earthly vessel's hunger to birth something for Him. Humble hearts and empty spiritual wombs always fulfill heaven's hunger for available vessels to hug hurting humanity. Hannah met both of heaven's requirements to get its attention; hunger and emptiness!

However, to activate God's favor upon her life she revealed her hunger and spiritual emptiness by a tremendous act. What did she do?

She offered God worship. Her worship was not limited to her temple attendance, sacrifices or her gut-wrenching prayer time (I Samuel 1:1-6). Hannah's worship time was not based on giving God ordinary expressions of thanksgiving, praise or circumstantial fasting. Her worship can be traced back to the bench mark of worship first mentioned in the Book of Genesis.

True Worship

Samuel was birthed out of an attitude and spirit of worship. The very word worship, when mentioned in any context produces various images and ideas within every one's mind. Some of these thoughts may be correct, while on the other hand some may be totally crazy or radical.

The Hebrew word ***Shachah,*** which was translated into the English word ***Worship*** according to Strong's Exhaustive Concordance of the Bible #7812 means ***'to depress, i.e. prostrate (especially. Reflex. In homage to royalty or God):-bow (self)***

down, even crouch, make to stoop, to WORSHIP.'

The first verse in the Book of Genesis, where this word is used, is out of the mouth of Abraham. He didn't use it in connection with a musical cord, beat, sound or a song unto the Lord, which is exactly what the Church has mistakenly labeled as worship.

Abraham, our father of the faith heard the voice of the Lord tell him to take his son and head to Mt. Moriah and offer him as a sacrifice. He obeyed the Word of the Lord, and when he arrived at the place God wanted, he told his servants the following: "***stay here with the donkey while I and the boy (Isaac) go over there. We will WORSHIP and then we will come back to you"*** (Gen. 22:5). What was Abraham's form of worship to God? If it was not playing of a tambourine, the stringing a harp, or the clash of cymbals, what did he do which he and God considered as worship? Abraham simply offered God what was priceless in his life, Isaac his son of promise (Gen. 17:19).

True worship is surrendering to God what we consider priceless to us. However, we don't choose what we offer. God told Abraham what He wanted. God will always inform us what He desires from us in worship.

Once we, the Bride of Christ, embrace this kingdom truth, we will be more than willing to submit to God what He considers priceless in this hour, and then we too will be favored by God.

The Vow

"O Lord Almighty, if you will only look upon your servant's misery and remember me, and not forget your servant but give her a son, then I will give him to the Lord or all the days of his life…"

(I Samuel 1:11)

Like most desperate believers when things seem like they are not turning out for our good we want to make a deal with God. Hannah is no exception to this truth. Prior to becoming pregnant with Samuel she made a vow. Along with the vow of life long service unto the Lord she promised, ***"…no razor will ever be used on his head."***

When a woman has a healthy pregnancy and is ready for delivery, the first thing seen of the new life exiting the narrow birth canal is the Head!

This is true as it pertains to the barren bride's children of leadership being birthed within this generation.

It is considered to be a troubled birth if the baby attempts to enter the world buttock or feet first. It is called a breached birth, and if possible the doctor must cause the baby to turn around while still in the womb.

The Church had birthed too many buttock and feet first ministries that placed the Church in the 'Dark Ages" and religious bondage.

Hannah's vow to the Lord regarding Samuel's hair was a Nazarene prophetic proclamation declaring what she will birth, honor and demonstrate apostolic authority (Numbers 6:5).

The barren bride's new breed of leadership will be a sign and wonder of total consecration to the Lord.

Unlike King David's son Absalom, whose appearance was outwardly glorious, nevertheless he was not able to walk in holy separation to God even when he did not cut his hair (I Samuel 14:25-26).

The Church within this hour can not afford spiritually to birth any more children who are only seasonally willing to grow their hair long and keep their vows on a part time basis.

The barren bride's children of leadership like Samuel must allow the strands of their hair (anointing, conduct, behavior and godly character) to grow and be seen as hope.

The world must see again the Church's outward signs that we are morally willing to take responsibility for being the light bearers in a dark time again.

The temporary rise of an Absalom spirit will always be defeated by its own ungodly ambitions, unstable commitment to godliness, and the need for self-glorification (I Sam. 18:9-10).

Only through wombs of worship will the Church give birth to more Samuels, and not Absaloms. Yet, we must make and keep our vows to the Lord.

Weaning

Have you ever heard the famous commercial slogan, "Got Milk?" If you have, and you've been a committed Christian for more then 5 years then you are qualified to attest to the fact that the Church has been feasting on a lot of milk lately.

After Samuel's birth, his mother Hannah had to wean him from her milk (I Sam. 1:24-25).

The word weans means *'to accustom to do without the mother's milk, to disengage from any habit.'* It was Hannah's responsibility, not God's, to initiate and cease the weaning process (I Sam. 1:21-23)!

I'm convinced that for years, too many sons and daughters of the Church have been participating in prolonged weaning processes. This produced unnatural dependency upon wombs (Churches, ministries, fellowships, etc.) that birthed them, as opposed to cleaving to the God that created them.

As a result of this, the Church had released to a hurting world a generation of "Spiritual Forrest Gumps", who are confused when the crises of life arrive at their doorstep.

Too many have been trained to run and jump in the lap of comfortable Christianity, while crying out, "Mamma, Got Milk?"

However, this is not true as it pertains to the spiritual Hannahs of this hour. These barren brides are determined that what they birth will know how to get life's nourishment from God, Who is also known as *"El Shaddai."*

The name *El Shaadai* has an awesome definition, which possesses a nourishing, mothering connotation. It means, *"The Breasty One."*

The Weaned Apostle

I believe the apostle John was spiritually *weaned* properly; therefore he didn't depend upon the other disciples' assumptions, suggestions and opinions or was willing to be a victim of other phobias.

It is very interesting that during the most critical meeting Jesus ever held with the twelve disciples it was the *weaned* one that the other disciples looked to be a conduit to ask Jesus their lives most troubling question.

Why did Peter, the disciple who possessed the revelation of Who Jesus the Christ is, did not ask Jesus himself? (Matt. 16:13-19). Rather, Peter was the one who asked John to question Jesus about who would be their betrayer (Jn.13:24).

John as a weaned man of God possessed two important elements within his life that qualified him to ask Jesus about His betrayer, and expect to receive an answer. The first thing he had was a revelation about Jesus.

The word revelation means *'illumination. God illuminates reveals, and informs of necessary knowledge.'* John knew who Jesus was and loved Him.

The second thing that John possessed, that the other disciples did not have, went beyond a revelation about Jesus.

What was it? Did the disciples consider John's talent to speak greater than theirs? Or maybe John had a reputation for casting out more demons, or ministering under a greater anointing for healing the sick then the others during their evangelistic campaigns (Lk. 10:1)?'

No! John had something greater than a revelation, spiritual gifts and power over satanic powers. He had a relationship with El Shaddia.

When believers are *weaned* timely in love they will make a smooth transition into total dependency upon the bosom of the Breasty One (Jesus Christ).

Peter and the other disciples knew that John found favor, comfort, assurance and a personal attachment to truth (Jesus). Therefore, that is why Peter had John talk to Jesus for them.

A revelation about God is never greater than a relationship with God. This is especially true whenever an answer is needed regarding life's troubling questions.

Apostle John asked Jesus the following question, ***"Lord, who is it that will betray you?"*** (Jn. 13:21-25).

John's relationship with Jesus the Christ led to the placement of his head upon the bosom of the Breasty One to hear the heartbeat of God. John did not just ask the question of the hour, but he also got the Son of God to give him the answer (Jn. 13:26).

This is why the Hannahs of this hour are refusing to birth Absaloms that refuse to submit to the weaning process. No longer will the Church live by Forrest Gump mother's philosophy of life. What was her philosophy? She told her lap dependent son, ***"Life is like a box of chocolates, you never know what you're going to get."***

Whenever the Church becomes spiritually flaky, God has always raised up some spiritual children of Issachar who understood the times and knew what they should do (I Chron. 12:32).

The current weaned leadership of the barren bride is totally committed *'to disengage from any habit or hindrances.'*

Yet, some of our gospel generals of old became irrelevant and frustrated in their last days because of the behavior of some of their spiritual sons and daughters they delayed weaning.

Unlike the Apostle John, too many spiritual Hophnies and Phinehases are working in the ministry and preaching behind pulpits (I Sam. 2:22-25).

Due to John's successful weaning process Jesus placed the future of the woman that weaned him into the hands of John's care and well being (Jn.19:26-27).

Today God is asking the Church an important question. The question is;

"Like John, can He trust us with the spiritual womb (The Church) that will produce sons and daughters of God which need to be weaned and properly released to the world?"

After Hannah completed her parental obligations to Samuel, he was ready to begin his journey into leadership.

The barren bride's children of leadership must be trained in two areas. These areas are the following:

The Secret of Servanthood.

The First Kick of Confirmation or Crisis?

Chapter Six

The Secret of Servanthood

Psalm 37:7

"Rest in the Lord, and WAIT patiently for Him…"

The first area of testing for the barren bride's children of leadership will be their willingness to submit to a pre-ordained position which most Christians seek to avoid at all cost.

The rumors and facts regarding this divine placement have caused massive confusion, ineffectiveness in true evangelism.

This ministry has been one of the main causes for church splits within the last 100 years. What type of ministry is this that vast majority of Christians hate with a heated passion?

Could it be the nursery ministry? How about the custodial ministry or the parking lot ministry? No! It is not that easy. Many who walked away from this particular placement, within the kingdom of God, departed with sadness, anxiety and anger with the Lord. This kind of divine position causes our hidden character blemishes to be seen, despite our greatest attempts to mask them. This ministry is what I call, ***'The Waiting Room Ministry.'*** Let me tell you a story how God revealed this particular ministry to me.

Waiters, Waitresses or Worries

One afternoon while dining in a restaurant, prior to one of my prophetic encounter meetings in Landover, Maryland, I had this awesome encounter with God and some of His people.

I was dining alone in a restaurant as I sensed the Spirit of the Lord greatly. I stopped eating and started surveying the restaurant seeking what or who the Lord wanted me to see? Immediately my attention was drawn to five waiters and waitresses performing their duties at various tables.

As I was watching them, I noticed that all of them were very gracious, polite and professional while conversing and serving the various customers they were assigned.

However, less than three fourths of them remained smiling when they left the tables to place their customer's orders. Then, I noticed that only one waitress continued to smile throughout the time of serving others.

This waitress was pregnant, and it seemed like she was ready to deliver her baby within seconds. She didn't move as swiftly as the others, nor did her food stained uniform fit loosely like theirs. Regardless, she possessed a great graciousness upon her life, and it was evident as she served people with an expression of endearment.

As I continued to observe her serve a party of six, I over heard several comments made regarding her due date for delivery, and how it must be very hard serving tables in her condition

The waitress gave them a radiant smile and said, "Yes, I'm due soon. But until then, I'll keep doing what I love to do, which is serving people." As she departed their table with her ordering pad in her left hand heading toward the kitchen doors, she gently began rubbing her belly with her right hand, while still displaying that awesome smile.

I knew at that very moment that God wanted me to be a financial blessing to her and the soon arrival of the new addition to her family. I waited until she returned with her parties' beverages and I got her attention. She arrived at my table with that glorious smile and she said, "Sir, how can I be of service to you?

I informed her that I was not a weirdo, but the Lord wanted to be a blessing to you today. I asked her to open her hands, and I placed within her hands the amount God instructed me to give. After a few seconds of astonishment she asked if she could be seated with me for a moment. Before she was seated she started crying, thanking me and praising God with reckless abandonment. I became nervous that she was about to deliver her baby at that very moment at my table.

Repeatedly, she placed her hands upon her belly and shouted, "God is faithful to His Word. My God is faithful to His Word." I immediately placed a tip upon the table for my assigned waiter and started to leave, then she grabbed my left arm and stated, "Please don't leave sir, I'm OK, and I must tell you something. So please don't leave until I return from serving my assigned table their order." Reluctantly I agreed.

Within minutes she returned to my table, she had regained her composure and began to tell me her story.

She asked me my name and if I was an angel? I told her my name and that I was a follower of Jesus Christ as my Lord and Savior. She said, "Can I tell you my testimony?" I agreed and she begun to tell me how she gave her heart to the Lord eight months ago.

One week after she accepted Christ, she discovered that she was pregnant. She said, "I'll probably never marry my baby's father." When she accepted Christ, she informed her boyfriend that she would no longer live with him, and they need to get married. However, until that time he needed to find his own place. She loved him and wanted them to serve Christ together, because he was a backslidden believer." However, much to her disappointment he angrily rejected her and her new relationship with Jesus Christ. She said I have not heard from him since.

With tears filling her eyes again she said, "I was not really surprised by his rejection, but I was hurt once again in my life by rejection. She continued to tell me her story and shared how she was raped by her stepfather at the age of 13.

She claimed her mother didn't believe her and she left home at the age of 14 and has been living on her own since. She just had her 18th birthday and is currently studying for her GED.

"I was so crushed when I discovered that I was pregnant one week after accepting Christ," She said, "I felt spiritually ashamed, dirty and angry with myself, and as a new Christian I struggled with the thoughts of abortion or adoption. Besides, I needed to get another job."

Then she went on to say, "I also had the constant thought of maybe I should not have placed such a demand on her boyfriend, at least, I would not be forced to deal with this alone." She paused to regain her composure and wipe tears from her eyes, then, she continued by saying "I was alone, scared and embarrassed."

She said, "Sir, I was confused, angry, desperate and afraid, and I didn't tell anyone, but I began to really cry out to the Lord. I can't call it prayer because I really didn't know how to pray yet, but I just poured out my heart to Jesus."

After two days of gut wrenching crying and dialogue with the Lord, He answered her with the following words in her heart, ***"If you serve Me and my people, I'll serve you and yours forever. Don't abandon nor abort what I have bestowed upon you."***

She said, "As a new babe in Christ I didn't know if this was from the Lord, or my imagination, so I wrote it down in my Bible and showed it to my pastor the next day.

The pastor confirmed it was a Word from God and then the pastor began to prophesy, ***"God will begin to place money in your hands through His children, which you don't know, and this will only*** *begin happening one month prior to your date of delivery."*

The waitress started weeping again and said, "Today, I'm one month away from my due date. Sir, you are the first person who gave me money for my baby in Jesus name that I don't know. I thank you oh so much, because the baby and I really can use this today. I don't have health insurance."

She got up from the table and gave me the biggest hug. As she was hugging me I began to prophesy regarding her son's destiny and purpose.

Much to our amazement while we were hugging and praising God customers within the restaurant, who were listening, got up from their tables and meals and begun placing money upon my table. Eventually, her co-workers were giving her hugs and placing their tips upon the table also, because they never heard her testimony.

A crowd waiting to be seated and served got out of line and placed 20 dollar bills and 50s upon the table for her too and got back in line. It was an unsolicited move of God during lunch time!

As the crowd got larger and larger I slipped out the door.

The Revelation in a Restaurant

When I returned to my hotel room I fell on my knees and started speaking in tongues and weeping under the presence of God for at least an hour.

When it seemed like God's presence lifted I was able to speak, so I asked God what was this all about? Immediately, the Lord spoke to my heart why He allowed me to experience what He did. He gave me the interpretation of the entire event.

He said ***"The restaurant was The Church, and the Waiters and Waitresses were my Leaders."***

He reminded me how every waiter and waitress were dressed in the same colored uniform and wore name tags that displayed the name of the restaurant and their names. They possessed the outward appearance of unity, but majority of them only had uniformity.

He said, ***"I've called all believers to minister (serve) others by occupying (taking residency) in the spirit of Christ as we patiently contribute to others well-being"*** (Matthews 25:35-36).

With apparent sadness in His tone He continued to say that His Church has forgotten the Secrets of Servant hood, which is only revealed in *'The **Waiting Room Ministry.**'* This is the ministry which every believer initially must serve in, but most dread with an unholy passion.

The Waiting Room

Throughout the entire restaurant episode, God accomplished several things in one moment, apart from the obvious. He showed me similarities between all leaders and the Waiters and Waitresses.

There were four kinds of leaders serving others with different motives, as it is within the 21st century Church.

The first group was Pretenders. They were acting polite, concerned, and warm and inviting with a smile. However, this was only done in an attempt to receive great financial gain from the ones they're serving.

The second group was the Lenders. They will lend you their attention and time because it is the restaurant owner's (God's) policy for employment and possible promotion. Yet it is not their personal passion to contribute to another's well-being without a price.

Lenders will allow you to borrow their talent, time and service, but with a high interest of return. They depend upon your hunger for an opportunity to fulfill their agenda.

The third group is the Contenders. They are hasty and overbearing with their service. Also they are always competing with others for tips (insights, information and recognition). They want massive quantity of service opportunities; but they really do not care about their quality of service.

Contenders only worry about one thing; getting their chance at being number one. They will always attempt to achieve this quest by cutting spiritual corners.

They possess no concern for who they may hurt or destroy in the process to obtain that goal. Contenders will not just fight other leaders, but they will fight God's way and His will for their lives.

Then lastly, there is the ***fourth group which is the Surrenders.*** This group of leaders comprehends their divine assignment and understands the privilege it is to service within the kingdom of God. They're a spiritually pregnant remnant within the Church that possesses awesome gifts, destinies and tremendous purposes, but they are willing to serve others up until it is their time to be served.

They are just like the pregnant waitress within the restaurant. They are waiting in the *Waiting Room* with great expectation and a smile.

Chapter Seven

The First Kick of Confirmation Or Crisis?

The Lord revealed to me the second test for the barren Bride's children of leadership. He said, "Regretfully, many within this hour are leaving the Waiting Room Ministry while they still have others they are assigned to serve."

As I pondered the Lord's words I realized that all of God's children do not start out in the Surrender group; they must go through the various trials, biblical chastisements, as well as life's storms to finally comprehend that they must wait upon their promise with patience.

The Lord Jesus had to be processed and proven that he was a part of the Surrender group, but without sin (Heb. 2:17-18). The Church is being seduced to embrace the spirits of Pretenders, Lenders and Contenders to leave our assigned tables of servant hood prematurely due to a misinterpretation of what I call the ***"First Kick of Confirmation or Crisis."***

What is the first kick of confirmation or crisis? It is when potentially great vessels for God are made aware of their divine deposit by experiencing the first kick of anointing, gifting, talents and ability within their spiritual wombs.

However, far too many of us mistakenly have interpreted the first kick as an indication it is time to birth a vision, mission or dream, when in all actuality it is only a confirmation of what God has promised regarding callings, gifts and talents for our lives and assignments.

Too many saints have taken their liberty in defining the first kick as divinely granted permission to start ministries, fellowships, denominations and churches.

Ignorant of the proper interpretation of the first kick, many have and will leave the waiting room ministry hastily before their assigned midwives (mentors/spiritual parents) of the Lord, can assist in getting them righteously prepped and positioned for delivery.

The spiritual midwives within this hour mission are to make sure their labor will not be grievous and no harm will come to the new birth (movement). Despite the overwhelming number of misinterpreted first kicks of confirmation, which has produced a generation in spiritual crisis, God rejoices over the spiritually pregnant saints who are not asking for pity, handouts, or to be replaced for a moment.

These saints are like the pregnant waitress in the restaurant. She understood her position and it was evident by how she wanted to please the people she was assigned to serve.

When a person embraces their waiting room experiences as a privileged, as opposed to a problem, they can receive things that only God can bestow; like being made pregnant with favor and saturated with a supernatural flow of divinely motivated ideas for the advancement of the Kingdom of God.

These rivers of blessings are for those who are aware of the Secret Servant hood.

Yes, it's sad to admit that within this time God rarely finds believers who are eager, excited or faithful to this assignment. I've always wondered why? Then I realized it is due to the unwillingness of many of us to endure the ear piercing silent seasons of waiting on God.

Servants in the natural must wait upon their employer's verbal directives, prior to any of their actions. The same is true regarding the Brides children of leadership.

This disdain of seemingly endless days, months or even years of pacing the floor in our minds, has caused some of God's potentially great leaders to lose consciousness of their faith. This occurs while trying to figure out God's reasoning for their delayed season of birthing.

Our enemy's strategy against the barren Bride's children of leadership many times is to attack our minds while God places us in the wait seasons of silence. He desires to deceive many of us to place a spiritual hangman's noose around our destiny and hope.

This method is not new, and the three cords that comprise this rope of no hope is not either. These three cords that are woven together are ***impatience***, ***worry*** and ***anger***.

The central demonic force that unites ***impatience*** and ***anger*** is **worry**! The root meaning for the word **worry** is derived from Germany origin, which means to ***'strangle and choke out.'***

Due to the misinterpretation of the first kick of confirmation regarding anointings, giftings, and callings several of God's most gifted believers become worried and attempt to manufacture their own miracle of untimely ministry.

Whenever the first kick is not discerned as a seed of confirmation, spiritual abortion is many chosen fate. However, regardless of several of the previous generation's successes they fall victim to hastiness, impatience and to self-servant hood.

Now is the time for the Barren Bride's children of emerging leadership to learn from previous generation's successes and failures.

Apostle Paul addressed this principle within his letter to the Church at Corinth, ***"Now these things were examples"(Cor. 1:6***). After passing the first two training sessions the third one is essential for choosing who will walk with them in the next move of God.

Chapter Eight

Godly Leadership Selection Processes

(Exodus 18:13-17)

"And it came to pass on the morrow that Moses sat to judge the people: and the people stood by Moses morning unto evening. And when Moses' father in law saw all that he did to the people, he said, What is this thing that thou thyself doest to the people? Why sittest thou thyself alone, and all the people stand by thee from morning unto even? And said unto his father in law, Because the people come unto me to enquire of God. When they have a matter, they come unto me; and I judge between one and another, and I do make them know the statues of God and his laws. And Moses' father in law said unto him, The thing that thou doest is not good."

Moses, throughout the first forty years of his life, prior to God's call, never really had a godly male mentor. Like many within this generation, godly male mentors, role models or natural and spiritual fathers are missing. The barren Bride's Children of

Leadership will need godly male mentors to help navigate them through this world to fulfill their destiny.

Moses was blessed to inherit a father in law who served as a godly male mentor after 40 years of living in Egypt without one. His name was Jethro. The scriptures reveal that after Moses delivered the children of Israel out of Egyptian captivity he became their pastor within the wilderness.

Moses' constant efforts to go to God on their behalf for numerous needs, selfish requests and provide counseling for the multitude were quite overwhelming.

During one of Jethro's visits, he discovered that Moses' was tired, weary and heavy burdened by the people's needs and request. Therefore, he gave Moses some godly advice to solve his dilemma. This advice is known as, ***'The Jethro Principle.'***

Our Heavenly Father winked at His Son's potential Bride's ignorance in the past, but He is no longer winking. Like Moses, many have attempted to run a one man/woman show within their ministry. Several have taken the position that if I do not do it, it will not get done, or it will not be done right.

Science Class Revelation

Once I over heard my son in his room on his laptop's webcam discussing a homework assignment with another student. Based on what I was able to hear they found it quite humorous that the media refers to famous people as ***'Stars**.'* This was so funny to them because during their science class they learned what a 'Star' is and what they are made of.

I chuckled and headed to my church office, when God spoke to my heart and said, ***"That is the problem I'm having with my Son's Bride. She wants to be a 'Star' instead of a wife!"***

Stars are fragments of a planet or a comet that broke away. They can be made of many different elements. The main two elements used in making a star are helium and hydrogen. Our sun is made up of 25% helium and 75% hydrogen.

Normally when we can see a star in the night sky it's become nothing more then a rock of hot gases ignited into flames falling to the earth.

Many times when there is not a godly mentor speaking into our lives, we take on the mind set of trying to become a 'star' in the kingdom. A lot of churches have locks on their doors, or their place of worship have become bingo halls or day care centers because leadership did not have or did not listen to their godly mentor's advice or counsel. They aspired to be stars instead of servants of the Most High God.

Moses' intentions were good, but if he would have continued to use his methods, he would have crashed and burned out before he ever got a chance to see the promise land.

The Jethro Principles for Leaders

(Exodus 18:21)

"Moreover thou shall provide out of all the people Able Men, such as Fear God, Men of Truth, Hating Covetousness."

Jethro advised Moses to have the people look among themselves for men that possessed four characteristics. The first one was ***Able Men***. These types of men are not very verbal, but they are production oriented. God wired them to perform under pressure, or no pressure, they are steady and dependable.

They totally rely upon God's ability within their lives to get any job done placed within their sphere of responsibility. They are normally not the most gifted, talented or anointed, but they are the most humble and effective.

The second characteristic was men that ***Fear God.*** The scriptures state, ***'The fear of the Lord is the beginning of wisdom' (Ps. 111:10).*** These kinds of men are full of godly wisdom and reverence for God. They are very patient and full of grace and love. Prayer is not what they do, it's who they are.

The third prototype leader attribute was ***Men of Truth.*** Truly, the Israelites then and the Church today, need ***Men of Truth*** from parking attendants to preachers. These men are not easily persuaded by false doctrines, trendy or popular movements within the Church that are not scripture based. They are not stagnate saints, but they base their lives on truth and nothing, or no one, will cause them to compromise their integrality.

Lastly, the Church has not transitioned from trying to keep up with the 'Jones Mentality.' There is such a spirit of lust for others blessings that it has laid the foundation for the general acceptance of the false doctrine that 'great gain' means godliness (I Tim. 6:3-7).

It is my prayer that the Lord sends us the Jethro(s) of this hour, who see what most ministries do not before they burn out being busy, but not effective.

The Elijah and Elisha Principles

(2 Ki. 2:1-1)

Every thing within this world has a purpose and a certain amount of time granted by God to fulfill that purpose. The Prophet Elijah was not immune to this spiritual law.

The Lord informed Elijah that he was going to establish a father/son relationship with the next prophet that would wear his mantle. God told him to go down to Shaphat's house and call his son Elisha to follow him in the ministry (I Ki. 19:19-21).

I find it interesting that God and the Prophet Elijah initiated this relationship. Not Elisha. Today, unlike Elisha, there are far too many young ministers attempting to choose their spiritual fathers like a buffet meal. No! The father chooses the son, not the other way around. This is why many times spiritual abuse occurs in relationships because God never ordained it.

Then Elijah demonstrates how to develop a godly relationship. Elijah takes Elisha on a spiritual journey to reveal his heart and mission. There are four spiritual pit stops Elijah makes prior to passing his mantle to Elisha.

The first pit stop is called **Gilgal**. It means ***'to cut off, roll away reproaches, willingness to cut off ungodly excess.'*** Elijah's admonition to Elisha was to remain in Gilgal (2 Ki. 2:2). All budding relationships will have a season of purging for maturity, yet the relationship can not remain in the purging stage all the time because eventually new healthy fruit will not have a chance to grow.

Several things occur at Gilgal which holds prophetic relevance to Elijah and Elisha developing relationship. Some of these revelatory historical events were:

The children of Israel ***No longer received Manna*** from heaven at Gilgal (Jos. 5:12). New godly relationships can not mature by living on miracles only. They must be in transition from seeking miracles to being someone else's conduit to miracles.

A second event was Joshua's instruction to the men who were born in the wilderness to ***circumcise themselves*** (Jos. 5:2-9). This was done so they would always remember the painful price associated with being a covenant people of God. This had to be done prior to entering the Promise Land, because only covenant people who understand the cost that Christ paid can have access to covenant promises.

Elijah wanted Elisha to understand that any new godly relationships must be willing to come into divine order, no matter what the personal cost. The barren Bride's children of leadership will pass through their spiritual Gilgals prior to receiving their mantle.

The third event was when the **Passover** was reinstituted there (Jos. 5:10). In order for godly relationships to thrive and flourish, there must be a time of reflection and honor for where and what God has brought each individual out of.

The Bride's children of leadership must never forget what God delivered them from, so they will not become prideful because of the awesomeness of their divine assignment.

Lastly, there was a Prophetic School (2 Ki. 4:38-4. Elijah wanted Elisha to understand who and what he was becoming. What was he becoming? ***A Prophetic Voice of God***.

True identification is easily obtained within a prophetic flow atmosphere. All godly relationships need to have a prophetic covering and guidance especially during the infancy of the relationship. The Bride's children of leadership will live a prophetic edge to their existence.

When there is not a prophetic word regarding the future of a new godly relationship, there will always be the uncertainty of that relationship's validity.

Yet, along with the need for a word from God, there must be an awareness of the adversary use of the spirit of divination. Many times this spirit may pretend to be a prophetic word from God. Several previous great leaders of past revivals fell victim to these voices that sound like God, but they were not. Sadly, therefore the moves of God ceased prematurely because decisions were made based upon false words of direction.

But today, like during the Apostle Paul's ministry, the Bride's children of leadership will face the same dilemma, as Paul, the discernment of these false voices must be identified and confronted (Acts 16:16-18).

Without a true Word from God, the survival of a new godly relationship is fatal. Therefore, symbolically speaking, Gilgal is the painful process of being transparent and vulnerable during the courtship season of a new godly relationship.

Elijah's second pit stop is called, **'Bethel.'** It means ***'House of God.'*** It represents the place of devotion to God and His ways. It is during this time at Bethel, potential godly relationships are challenged to dedicate and consecrate themselves to the betterment of each other.

Monumental events happen when a new godly relationship is within its ***Bethel Season***. Some of these events are:

Jacob saw the vision of the ladder (Gen. 28:10-22; 31:13). Bethel is the place where God's presence is tangible and decisions must be made there to live a secular or scared life before God.

The tabernacle was built in Bethel (Jg. 2:18, 31; 21:2). Therefore, Bethel also represents God's access to earth, and man's access to heaven. The Bride's children of leadership must be willing to allow the new godly relationship to develop from a horizontal state, based upon the five senses, to a vertical one, established by a revelation from God.

Without a Bethel encounter, all new potential godly relationships will be limited to a fleshy existence at best.

The third pit stop was **Jericho**. It means ***'to see, comprehend and insight.'*** It represents a place of illuminated breakthrough. An awesome example of this truth is found in **'Blind Bartimaeus'** encounter with Jesus. Bartimaeus is healed from his blindness on the highway near Jericho (Mk. 10:46-52; Matt. 2:29-34; LK. 18:35-43).

Nevertheless, prior to his healing Bartimaeus had to become verbally violent in his attempt to get Jesus' attention as he was passing him by.

As Jesus journeyed through Jericho, the city of sight, comprehension, and conflict, Bartimaeus was positioned next to that city which represented what he wanted, sight, comprehension and breakthrough. He got what he needed from the Lord Jesus.

Many new godly relationships may be right at the brink of what they need for their relationships to be whole and complete. But we must remember that this is only accomplished after a time of ***conflict*** and ***struggle.***

This is especially true when there is an attempt to obtain ***insight, comprehension*** and ***truth*** regarding each other. The Bride's children of leadership will learn how to gain access to Jesus despite ***contrary words, thoughts, opinions*** and ***deeds.***

Whenever there are ungodly blind spots regarding a new godly relationship, problems can not prevail if our passionate pursuing persistence is based upon capturing God's vision.

Then the final pit stop is **Jordan**. Symbolically Jordan represents three vital stages.

(1) ***Spiritual Death***

(2) ***The Supernatural***

(3) ***The Double Portion.***

The Jordan is a type and shadow of Spiritual Death (2 Ki. 5:1-14; Matt. 3:6) throughout scriptures. Water baptism was performed there to symbolize the death of the 'old' man prior to accepting Christ as Lord and Savior. Then the emerging from the water was a demonstration of 'New' life in Christ.

Elijah led Elisha to the Jordan so Elisha could make a final decision to embrace this new godly relationship. This decision required more than Elisha boiling his oxen of the past vocation or career (I Ki. 19:19-21), it required a death to his vision, plans and goals for his life, apart from God's approval.

Along with the Jordan being a place of spiritual death it also represents a place of ***The Supernatural*** (Jos. 3;4; 5:1; Ps. 114:3). Elijah's drying up the Jordan River so he and Elisha could cross was evidence of the Supernatural power of God within his life. Interestingly, Elijah did not reveal to Elisha the anointing that was upon his life while journeying through Gilgal, Bethel or Jericho. Why? Because whenever fostering new godly relationships it is always best to test if that person desires the relationship because of their love for you, and not what they see possess (Acts 8:17-22).

The Double Portion ((Ki. 2:9-11). The true fruit of a godly relationship is when a mentor initiates the conversation regarding inheritances. Elijah asked Elisha first, "What can I do for you when I'm gone." Elisha did not act like the youngest son in Jesus' parable the Prodigal Son (Lk. 15:11-19).

The Bride's children of leadership must be very careful who they partner with during this season. They must disassociate from servants pretending to be partners, sons and daughters. They will be identified by their conversation and actions, which will always be centered on what they are going to get for their alliance.

Elisha told Elijah what he desired, it was a double portion. However, Elijah's instructions to qualify for the **Double Portion** were interesting. Elijah said, ***'Thou hast asked a hard thing: nevertheless,***

if thou 'SEE' me when I am taken from thee; but if not, it shall not be so' (2 ki. 2:1).

Elijah was telling Elisha if you ***SEE*** this calling (relationship) the way God and I intended it for you, then you will receive the **Double Portion**.

Many ministry mantles are being bestowed upon relationships that are doing it God's way. Unfortunately, today, several mantles are being taken by carnal ***Servants*** (laborers for hire) as oppose to ***Sons*** and **Daughters** (true inheritors) of the respective Houses (ministries, churches, etc. Ps. 127).

Due to the fact that ***'Servants'*** are not privileged to know (acquainted, intimate or conscious) the vision of the House, so they create ***'Di (two) – Vision' by casting strange missions and visions before the people.*** The Bride's children of leadership must know who they are laboring with in order for the anointing to rest upon the right visionaries.

The last principle I desire to address is a prophetic directive for the barren Bride's children of leadership that is seen in the commission of King Jehu.

The Jehu Principles for Selecting Godly Relationships

(2 Kings 10:15-16)

"…And when he was departed thence, he lighted on Jehonadab the son of Rechab coming to meet him: and saluted him, and said to him, Is thine heart right, as my heart is with thy heart? And Jehonadab answered, Is it. If it be give me thine hand. And he gave him his hand; and he took him up to him into the chariot. And he said, Come with me, and see my zeal for the Lord. So they made him ride in his chariot."

Marriages, friendships, business partners, prayer partners and staffers all have at least one thing in common, relationships. The hottest selling books on the New York Times' Best Sellers list are books that address topics regarding, 'How to Get Money' and others are books on 'Relationships!' It seems like everyone has their opinions on how to establish or maintain good relationships.

We've been blessed to have several excellent Christian authors who address this topic also like Dr. James Dobson and Gary Chapman to name a few. Yet, the secular world refuses to be silent regarding this subject also. Therefore, comedians; like Roseanne Barr, Steve Harvey and Dr. Bill Cosby, along with various actors, politicians and professional athletes have penned their insights regarding relationships.

Let's view some more time proven methods and principles found within the godly quest and mission of King Jehu.

(2 Kings 9:1-3)

"And Elisha the prophet called one of the children of the prophet, and said unto him, Gird up thy loins, and take this box of oil in thine hand, and go to Ramothgilead: And who thou comest thither, look out there Jehu the son of Jehoshaphat the son Nimshi, and go in, and make him arise up among his brethren, and carry him to an inner chamber; Then take the box of oil, and pour it on his head, and say, Thus saith the Lord, I have anointed the King over Israel. Then open the door, and flee, and tarry not."

Like the barren Bride's children of leadership, Jehu was made king for a particular divine assignment:

(2 Kings 9:7)

"And thou (Jehu) shalt smite the house of Ahab thy master, that I may avenge the blood of my servants of the Lord, at the hand of Jezebel."

Regardless that King Jehu was trained, skilled, anointed, appointed and released to fulfill God's desire, he could not accomplish it without relationships:

(2 Kings 9:30-33)

"And when Jehu was come to Jezreel, Jezebel heard of I; and she painted her face, and tired her head, and looked out at a window. And as Jehu entered in at the gate, she said, 'Had Zimri peace, who slew his master? And he lifted up his face to the window, and said, Who is on my side? Who? And there looked to him two or three eunuchs. And he said, Throw her down. So they threw her down: and some of her blood was sprinkled on the wall, and on the horses: and he trod her under foot."

Jehu to fulfill God's desire and his purpose had to team up with eunuch servants within Ahab and Jezebel's palace. The scriptures reveal that Jehu never laid a hand upon Jezebel because he had the ability to incorporate different people to support his assignment. He was able to work with eunuchs within the palace.

What are eunuchs? They were male servants who had no male reproductive organ. Their conditions were a result of one of the four following reasons:

(1) A birth defect.
(2) Unfortunate accident.
(3) Their masters castrated them so they would not be a sexual threat to the master's wives and concubines that they were assigned to serve.
(4) A religious belief.

The scriptures do not provide any details how these particular men became eunuchs. Yet, spiritually speaking, King Jehu discerned their lack of alliance to King Ahab and his wife Jezebel. Similarly, the barren Bride's children of leadership must possess the ability to recognize and touch the penned up passions of a spiritual orphaned generation. Too many within this generation are the victims of emotional and spiritual castration by life's situations, bad decisions and destructive relationships.

Despite King Jehu's success over Jezebel, his divine assignment was not complete. God also wanted King Ahab's male lineage to be destroyed off the face of the earth forever:

(2 Kings 9:7-9)

"And thou shalt smite the house of Ahab thy master, that I may avenge the blood of my servants the prophets, and the blood of all the servants of the Lord, at the hand of Jezebel. For the whole house of Ahab shall perish: and I WILL CUT FROM AHAB HIM THAT PISSETH AGAINST THE WALL, AND HIM THAT IS SHUT UP AND LEFT IN ISRAEL…"

As Jehu, this barren Bride's children of leadership will learn how to select various people to join them in fulfilling God's vision. Let us look at what I call ***'The Jehu Principles for Selecting Godly Relationships.'***

During King Jehu's voyage to Samaria to accomplish God's desire, he encounters Jehonadab coming to meet him.

The First Principle

(It's a Matter of the Heart)

2 Ki.10:15 – Jehu saluted him, and said to him, ***"Is thine HEART right, as my HEART is with thy HEART?"*** Jehu's first principle for establishing godly relationships is to perceive the potential person's heart toward him and God's mission for his life.

Whatever a person's heart is fixed upon, that is where their loyalties and treasures rest (Matt. 6:21). Too many believers fail this test because they take people at their word as proof of their devotion. We must never forget that our hearts reveal what or whom we trust, even when our lips may say otherwise. Therefore, Jehu did not take Jehonadab's word only, he wanted evidence. Also the Bride's children of leadership can not afford to be victims of leaven filled words of flattery within this hour.

The Second Principle

(Give Me Your Hand)

(V.15) Jehu replied by saying, ***"...If it be, give me thine HAND."*** As the barren Bride's children of leadership are chosen by God to birth His new movement within the earth, God will require more then verbal expressions to demonstrate heart felt commitment.

Proof of a person desire to covenant with you for a godly purpose is their willingness to submit their **HAND** (abilities, talents, gifting, resources, etc.) within your God controlled influence.

Always ask for the **Hand** prior to giving your **Heart.**

The Third Principle

(Welcome to My Vision Voyage)

As Jehu continued his dialogue with a potential godly partner, he offered him the opportunity to join him in his chariot. **Chariots** in scripture have various prophetic meanings, such as ***(power, speed, transportation in warfare and elevation— Ps. 2:7; 14:3; Zec. 6:1-2; Isa. 66:15; 2 Ki. 2:11).***

However, Jehu shows us that we should wait until we have seen that person's **HEART** and received their **HAND** prior to inviting them to join us in our field of dreams or a God ordained assignment.

The offering of the **HAND** is not a one way street. Jehu also had to make an offer of what was in his Hand too. But, this only occurred after Jehonadab **HAND** was submitted. Then Jehu offered his ***HAND of ELEVATION*** to Jehonadab to enter into his chariot once he was fully confident of Jehonadab's potential loyalty.

The barren Bride's children of leadership are required within this hour to perceive **Hearts** and receive and extend **Hands.**

The Fourth Principle

(Come and See)

Lastly, Jehu after taking Jehonadab through the various tests, he finally tells him, ***"Come with me and See my zeal for the Lord."*** **(V.16).**

For years the Church has done this backwards. In the past we have told and shown people our **zeal** ***(Vision)*** for the Lord without discerning if their **Heart** and **Hand** are with us. This fatal spiritual deed led to great movements of God expiring prior to obtaining God's complete purpose for their existence.

Revival flames were quenched, denominations were split and God's voice seemed absent because many spiritual leaders did not discern the Body of Christ properly (I Cor. 11:26-30).

Whenever spiritual leadership does not properly discern God's divine placement of His members (5-fold offices, eyes, ears, etc. saints) they become avenues for spiritual weakness and sickness.

During this season we can not afford for members to be placed incorrectly within the Body of Jesus. The barren Bride's children of leadership can not afford to enter hastily into covenant relationships with disguised spiritual Judases.

I'm convinced that these principles will assist in revolutionizing the Church from childish behavior and youthful indiscretions into the Bride that Christ Jesus awaits.

All these principles; Jethro, Elijah/Elisha and Jehu showed how to select godly relationships that will allow saints/leaders to share their spirit, vision and life. The barren Bride's children of leadership will learn how to prayerfully discern potential godly relationships while moving toward the fulfillment of God's mandate.

Prophetically speaking, I see a remnant of believers being used by God within this hour that are viewed by the Church world the most unlikely. They may be our spouses, sons, daughters, grand-children, next door neighbors, friends, foes and even ourselves. Their selection by God is due to their barren plights of the past.

Ready or not here comes the barren Bride's children of leadership. Some of the signs of their arrival will be their non-traditional, morally un-compromising, and eager to see God's glory return back to the Houses of God.

It is time for the knowledge of God's glory to be revealed throughout the world. Are you prepared to go through the barren Bride's children of leadership process?

If you are, then keep in mind that the Heavenly Father's cry has been proclaimed, ***'When the Bride is Barren,'*** His Son will appear dressed for a wedding ceremony, which will be second to none other in the universe…

'Come Lord Jesus, Come your Bride awaits!'

11286547R00063

Made in the USA
Charleston, SC
12 February 2012